FRESH HERB

Jane Wilson Morton
and
Marianne K. Preston

POCKET COOKBOOK

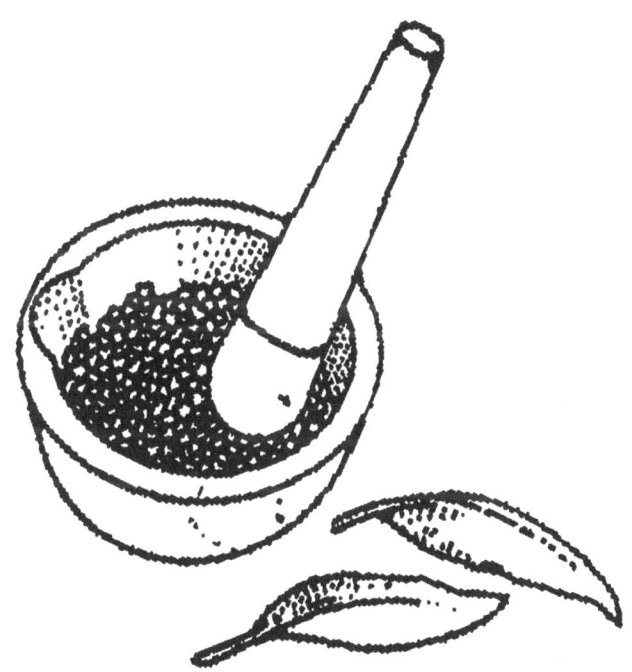

The Brick Tower Press ®
1230 Park Avenue, New York, NY 10128
Copyright © 1996
Jane Wilson Morton & Marianne K. Preston
All rights reserved under the International and
Pan-American Copyright Conventions.
Printed in the United States by J. T. Colby & Company, Inc., New York.
No part of this publication may be reproduced, stored in a retrieval system,
or transmitted in any form or by any means, electronic, mechanical,
photocopying, recording, or otherwise, without the prior written
permission of the publisher.

Morton, Jane Wilson
Preston, Marianne K.
Neat Pocket Cookbooks, Herb
First Edition, June 1996
Includes Index
ISBN 1-883283-10-8 softcover

NEAT FACTS ABOUT HERBS

Herbs are the jewels in the crown of the simplest as well as the most complicated recipes. Herbs come to the rescue when searching for a natural way to enhance flavor while keeping within the guidelines of a well-balanced diet. With their variety of flavors the cook can cut back on salt and fats and easily fall into line with the suggestions of nutrition and health professionals.

In general, herbs grow in temperate climates and the flavor oils reside in the leaves of the plants. Spices come from tropical climes and are the root, bark, seed, berries, and buds of various plants and trees. Herbs and spices are frequently used together like chili powder and curry powder. We have a recipe for making Chili Powder on page 6. Try it!

This collection of recipes uses commonly grown and easily accessible garden herbs found throughout American folklore from the Pilgrims to modern times. In 1796, Amelia Simmons wrote, in the First American Cookbook, "Garlicks, tho' used by the French, are better adapted to the use of medicine than cooking." How tastes have changed in 200 years! Simmons also designated "the seven herbs useful in cookery" as thyme, sweet marjoram, savory, sage, parsley, pennyroyal, and horseradish. All but pennyroyal are still popular.

Herbs have a worldly heritage that includes the renowned "herbs of Provence" - rosemary, thyme, and tarragon - the heart and soul of French Provincial and Mediterranean cooking. Sesame (benne) seeds came to the Americas through the African slave trade and we enjoy them regularly on cookies, cakes, and bagels. Meanwhile, travelers to the Americas took indigenous

American seasonings, like allspice berries, and sweet and hot peppers, back to their native lands.

Cilantro, alias coriander and Chinese parsley, seasons foods in the American southwest, as well as in Mexico, China, and India. Basil, one of our favorites, came into widespread use in the United States after World War II when American servicemen brought it home from Europe. Now it's a mainstay on American herb shelves, and is almost as available as parsley in the supermarket produce department.

An herb garden is a sensory garden. You rub the leaves and sniff the fragrance on your fingertips. You pinch a leaf and nibble to test the strength of the flavor. Seeing, touching, smelling, tasting; these are the senses that are stimulated as you bring an herb garden to fruition. Touch the savory, enjoy the aroma of mint and basil, and appreciate the delicate flavor of woodruff.

Our cookbook provides the cook with a delightful array of sensate recipes - from beverages, appetizers, and breads, to soups, vegetables, and desserts. Herbs play various roles in the makeup of a recipe. They can be subtle enhancers that lay back and give the main ingredient the lead role, as in Roasted Chicken with Pesto or Turkey Sausage. They can be the dominant flavor that maintains its own identity but blends with the main ingredient as in Roast Leg of Lamb with Garlic and Oregano or Tomatoes, Basil and Red Onion Rings. They can take over entirely and be the taste of the recipe as in Pesto Sauce or Cajun Mayonnaise.

We hope that each recipe you try entices you to try another and yet another. Perhaps you will be inspired to plant a few herbs or expand a present herb bed. You will start to think differently about flavoring your foods and be on your way to new culinary adventures. Let your taste buds be your major guide. Substitute one herb for another and experiment. Herbs, with their flavor and beauty, whether they come from the home garden, the greengrocer, or the supermarket, provide pleasure to the eye, nose, mind, and palate.

JANE WILSON MORTON & MARIANNE K. PRESTON

PLACES WHERE TOPICS BEGIN

Herbal Hints...4
Appetizers...7
Soups...9
Seafood...11
Meat...13
Poultry...15
Sauces...17
Vegetables...19
Salads & Dressings...21
Breads...23
Desserts...25
Beverages...27
Index...29

HERBAL HINTS

Good kitchen shears are the best utensil for gathering herbs from the garden as well as for snipping them into small pieces.

Use a less pungent herb seasoning for a weak flavored main ingredient in order to achieve a happy flavor balance.

If you're not sure of an herb's specific flavor, mix some with unsalted butter, let it stand for an hour, then spread on a plain cracker and taste.

To substitute dried herbs for fresh, use half the quantity called for in the recipe.

Coarse or woody stems of herbs should be discarded when chopping the leaves. Young, tender stems can be included.

To strip small leaves off stems (e.g. thyme), hold the sprig by the tender end and gently run your fingers along the stem toward the tough root end, pushing the leaves off as you go. The tender tip will break off and can be used.

Gather the herbs needed for the day early in the morning, when they are freshest. Rinse with cool water to clean, and stand stems in a glass of cold water until ready to use.

Basil leaves or other large leafy herbs, used in salad or as garnish, are best torn into pieces with the fingers to prevent discoloring.

To *chiffonade* large leaves like basil, stack several leaves one on top of the other, lay them on a board in front of you with the length of the leaves running left to right. Roll them into a tight cylinder and slice as thinly as you possibly can. You will have fine little shreds of basil.

The flowers of herbs are edible and make charming garnishes. Chive flowers can be used whole when garnishing or torn apart and scattered into a salad.

Almost all herbs make interesting teas. Mint, lemon verbena, thyme, sage, and bee balm (bergamot) are some you can use. Bergamot is a native American herb introduced to settlers by the Oswego Indians. Tea made from the leaves is called Oswego Tea. 2 teaspoons of crushed fresh herb steeped in 1 cup of boiling water for 5-10 minutes will produce a nice tea. Strain out the herbs.

Herb infused vinegars and oils are popular. Add herbs to warmed vinegar or oil, bottle and let sit for a couple of weeks, then enjoy their new flavor. Tarragon is one of the more popular herb vinegars, and a stalk of crushed lemon grass gives a subtle taste to oil or vinegar.

Maximum flavor is extracted when you add herbs to a sauté pan as you heat the oil or butter. For long, slow cooking, add herbs during the last 30 minutes of simmering.

Bay leaves are indigestible and should be removed before a dish is served.

The flavor of herb seeds like coriander, mustard, cumin, fennel, and sesame intensify if heated in a 300° F. oven for 3-5 minutes or in a non-stick skillet for 2-3 minutes. The same is true of nuts.

DRYING HERBS

The easiest method is to wash and dry a few stalks of the herb, tie them together at the stem end, and hang upside down in a dry, warm spot with good air circulation, out of direct sun.
OR
Wash and dry the herbs, strip the large leaves off the stems, dry the smaller stems whole. Spread out on a piece of screening where air can circulate on all sides freely. It takes about a week for them to dry. Turn the leaves regularly during the process.
OR
Microwave - check your microwave book for the best approach for your particular model.

OR
Oven method - spread clean leaves on a baking tray and place in a 200° F. oven for about 20 minutes or more. The dried herbs should retain some of their green color and be completely dry. Cool and place into clean jars.
Cap, label, and store in a cool, dark, dry place.

Dried herbs maintain peak flavor for about 6 months; so gauge your purchases according to the quantity you regularly use.

Fines Herbes are a blend of parsley, chervil, chives, and tarragon.

Bouquet Garni includes bay leaf, parsley, and thyme. The herbs may be tied in a little cheesecloth packet - OR you can use the parsley stem to tie around the bay leaf and thyme - OR you can place the herbs into the hollow of a 3-inch piece of outer stalk of celery, cover with a second piece, and tie them together. This technique allows the flavor of the herbs to permeate the soup or stew while providing a way to discard the herbs easily when you wish.

Barbecue Blend includes cumin, garlic, hot pepper, and oregano.

Remember that you must be the ultimate judge of how much seasoning you want in a particular dish. Start with a small amount, taste, add more if desired.

CHILI POWDER

1 teaspoon of cayenne pepper, 3 teaspoons of sweet paprika, 1 teaspoon of cumin powder, 1 teaspoon of ground coriander, 1/2 teaspoon of Mexican oregano, 1/4 teaspoon of allspice, a pinch of cloves. Combine all ingredients, mixing well.
Store in a cool place, in an airtight jar.
(The freezer and refrigerator are excellent for storage).

COTTAGE CHEESE WITH HERBS

❧ THINGS YOU NEED:

2 cups of cottage cheese
1 tablespoon of minced tarragon
1 tablespoon of minced flat leaf parsley
1 teaspoon of minced thyme
1 tablespoon of minced onion chives
1/2 teaspoon of coarsely ground black pepper
1/8 teaspoon of cayenne pepper (optional)
1/4 teaspoon of paprika
1 chive blossom, nasturtium,
or parsley sprig

HERE'S WHAT YOU DO:

In a medium bowl, combine the cottage cheese, tarragon, parsley, thyme, onion chives, black pepper, and cayenne pepper. Cover and chill for 3 or 4 hours or up to 3 days. Place in a serving dish; sprinkle with paprika and garnish with a chive blossom, nasturtium, or parsley sprig in the center. Serve with cut vegetables or triangles of toasted bread or crackers.

PARSLEY

MAKES 2 1/4 CUPS

TOAST CRISPS

🌿 THINGS YOU NEED:

1 round loaf of crusty bread
1 cup of minced oregano leaves
1 1/2 cups of shredded Parmesan cheese
1/2 cup of shredded, sharp Cheddar cheese
1/8 cup of olive oil
cayenne pepper (optional)

NOTE: These will hold for up to 2 weeks in a cool place. To increase the yield to 40 pieces cut each slice in half. Serve with cocktails, salads, or omelets.

HERE'S WHAT YOU DO:

Preheat oven to 350° F.

Quarter the loaf of bread and cut into 1/2-inch slices. Lightly toast the bread on both sides in a toaster or under a broiler. Place the toasted slices on a baking tray. Combine oregano, two cheeses, and olive oil. Spoon the cheese mix onto the bread, making sure the surface of the bread is covered. Sprinkle on cayenne pepper. Bake for 15 minutes in preheated oven or until cheese is crusty and golden.
Cool and store in tins until ready to serve.

MAKES ABOUT 20 SLICES

PEPPERS WITH SAGE

❧ THINGS YOU NEED:
1/3 cup of olive oil
1 clove of garlic, minced
2 tablespoons of minced sage leaves
1 tablespoon of minced oregano leaves
1 teaspoon of salt
1 1/2 teaspoons of ground pepper
2 medium red peppers, cored and sliced into thin slivers
1 medium green pepper, cored and sliced into thin slivers
1 medium yellow pepper, cored and sliced into thin slivers
1 large red onion, peeled and sliced into thin circles
sprigs of sage

HERE'S WHAT YOU DO:

Heat the olive oil in a large skillet. Add the garlic, sage, oregano, salt and pepper. Sauté 3 minutes. Add the peppers, sauté 5 minutes, stirring frequently. Add the onion, sauté 5 minutes or until limp. Peppers will remain fairly firm. Transfer to a serving dish and garnish with sprigs of sage.

NOTE: Serve warm as a side dish with roasts or fish or serve at room temperature as a salad or appetizer.

SERVES 3-4

CURRIED LENTIL SOUP

❧ THINGS YOU NEED:
6 tablespoons of olive oil
1 cup of diced onion
3/4 cup of diced carrots
1/2 cup of diced celery
2 cloves of garlic, minced
1 tablespoon of finely minced ginger
1/4 teaspoon of red pepper flakes (optional)
1/8 cup of curry powder
2 teaspoons crushed coriander seeds
1 tablespoon of crushed cumin seeds
1 tablespoon of minced oregano leaves
1/8 teaspoon of cayenne pepper
salt to taste
2 cups of lentils, rinsed
6 cups of water
1 to 1 1/2 cups of heavy cream or half and half
sour cream
chopped scallion

HERE'S WHAT YOU DO:
In a deep saucepan, heat the olive oil. Add the onion, carrots, and celery. Stir and sauté about 4 minutes. Add the garlic, ginger, pepper flakes, curry, coriander, cumin, oregano, cayenne pepper, and salt. Stir to combine and simmer for 5 minutes. Add the lentils. Stir to combine and simmer another 4 minutes. Add 6 cups of cold water. Cover and bring to a boil. Lower the heat and simmer, partially covered for about 45 minutes or until the lentils are tender. Cool and purée the soup in a food processor or blender until creamy. Transfer to a bowl, cover and refrigerate for at least one day. The soup will hold up to 4 days. If serving hot, reheat, add the amount of cream you prefer and heat through. If serving cold, stir cream into cold soup and serve. Garnish with a dollop of sour cream and a sprinkling of chopped scallions.

SERVES 6-8

CURRIED SCALLOPS

❧ THINGS YOU NEED:
4 tablespoons of sweet butter
1 bunch of scallions with tops, minced
1 large clove of garlic, minced
1 tablespoon of minced oregano leaves
1 teaspoon of minced tarragon leaves
1/4 cup of mild, medium, or hot curry according to your taste
20 large sea scallops (5 per person)
1 1/2 cups of heavy cream or half and half
salt and pepper to taste
extra scallion tops, minced

TARRAGON

HERE'S WHAT YOU DO:

In a large sauté pan, melt the butter until bubbly. Add the scallions and sauté for 5 minutes or until limp. Add the garlic, oregano, tarragon, and curry. Sauté 2 minutes and then add the scallops in 3 batches, sautéing each batch until just firm, about 5-7 minutes. Transfer them to a dish to keep warm. Add the heavy cream or half and half to the pan. Simmer until slightly thickened, about 10 to 15 minutes. Just before serving, add the scallops and simmer for 3 more minutes coating them well with the sauce.
Garnish with the extra scallion tops.

NOTE: *Serve with steamed rice and traditional curry garnishes; sliced bananas, peanuts, chutney, coconut, and raisins.*

SERVES 4

BAKED SHARK WITH BASIL

🌿 THINGS YOU NEED:

Marinade
1/4 cup of olive oil
1/2 cup of minced flat leaf parsley
1/4 cup of minced oregano leaves
2 scallions, minced with tops
1/8 teaspoon of red pepper flakes

4 shark steaks about 1 1/2-inches thick (swordfish, salmon, halibut or scrod are excellent substitutes)
2 tablespoons of olive oil
1 cup of large basil leaves
2 cloves of garlic, sliced
1 large onion, sliced
1 cup of peeled, diced tomatoes
1 teaspoon of black pepper
1 cup of white wine

HERE'S WHAT YOU DO:
Preheat oven to 350° F.

Two hours before cooking, combine the marinade ingredients. Coat the shark steaks, lay them in a pan, cover, and chill. When ready to cook brush olive oil on the bottom of a baking dish large enough to hold the steaks in one layer. Using one half of the basil leaves make a layer of leaves for the steaks. Place the steaks on top. Place the garlic and onion slices on top of the fish. Top with the remaining basil leaves and tomatoes. Sprinkle on the pepper and add the white wine. Bake in the lower portion of the oven for 30 to 40 minutes. Serve immediately with rice.

SERVES 4

THYME CRUSTED PORK CHOPS

🌸 THINGS YOU NEED:
2 cups of fine bread crumbs
1/3 cup of fresh thyme leaves
1 teaspoon of salt
1 teaspoon of ground pepper
2 cups of milk
4 large or 8 small pork chops,
1-inch thick
4 tablespoons of sweet butter
3 Granny Smith apples, peeled, cored and cut into
1/2-inch circles
4 sprigs of thyme or parsley

HERE'S WHAT YOU DO:
Preheat oven to 350° F.
Prepare a baking pan by lining with aluminum foil and adding a rack for baking. In a bowl wide enough to hold a chop, combine the crumbs, thyme, salt and pepper. Pour the milk into a similar bowl. Coat the chops with the milk, then heavily coat with the crumbs. Lay the chops on the rack and bake in a preheated oven for about 1 1/2 hours turning once until they are crisp on both sides. While the chops are baking melt the butter in a sauté pan until bubbly. Add the apple slices and sauté on both sides until slightly browned. Serve chops with a few overlapping slices of the apples, garnishing each with a
sprig of thyme or parsley.

SERVES 4

ROAST LEG OF LAMB
WITH GARLIC AND OREGANO

✿ THINGS YOU NEED:

3 to 4 pounds of shank half leg of lamb
3 cloves of garlic, peeled and thinly sliced
2 tablespoons of olive oil
salt and freshly ground black pepper
1 teaspoon of dried oregano
1 lemon, cut in half, seeds removed
4 stalks of celery, trimmed

HERE'S WHAT YOU DO:
Preheat oven to 325° F.

Remove lamb from refrigerator 1/2 hour before roasting. Wipe lamb with a clean, damp cloth. Trim off any excess fat. With a small, sharp, pointed knife, make a slit in the lamb 1/2 to 1-inch deep. Slip a slice of garlic into the slit. Continue to make slits and insert garlic all around the roast, 10-12 times. Rub the roast all over with olive oil. Sprinkle with salt and pepper and the dried oregano. Squeeze lemon juice over all. Lay the celery stalks in a suitable size roasting pan. Place the lamb on top with the fat side up. Roast, allowing about 16 minutes per pound for medium rare, about 21 minutes for well done. When the roast is done remove it from the oven and let stand about 10 minutes before carving. Serve with mint sauce or mint jelly. Garnish with fresh mint leaves.

SERVES 4-6

ROAST CHICKEN WITH PESTO

BASIL

🌿 THINGS YOU NEED:
3 to 4 pound whole chicken
1/2 cup of Pesto Sauce, (see page 17), made without the cheese
salt
2 tablespoons of butter, melted

HERE'S WHAT YOU DO:
Preheat oven to 350° F.
Wash chicken inside and out and pat dry. Salt the cavity and the skin, rubbing it in as much as possible. Use a wooden spoon handle and carefully insert it under the breast skin. Loosen the skin from the breast flesh, then work the handle into the thigh and leg areas as far as you can. Use a teaspoon to insert the pesto between the skin and the flesh. Push a spoonful in as far as you can and spread it around. Coat all the loosened areas. Tie the legs and wings so they stay close to the chicken's body. Brush chicken with melted butter and roast for 30 minutes. Baste with pan drippings. Roast another 30 minutes or until skin is crisp and brown and thigh juices run clear. Remove from oven and let stand for 10 minutes before carving.
Serve with pasta or rice and a salad.

NOTE *If desired, you can spread pesto under the skin of cut up pieces and broil or bake them. This chicken is also delicious at room temperature, served at a buffet or picnic.*

SERVES 4

TURKEY SAUSAGE

❧ THINGS YOU NEED:

1 tablespoon of vegetable oil
1 small clove of garlic, minced
1/2 cup of finely chopped onion
1 pound of ground turkey
1/2 to 1 teaspoon of red pepper flakes (depending on your taste)
1/4 teaspoon of cayenne pepper
1/4 teaspoon of salt
1 teaspoon of finely minced fresh sage
1/2 cup of plain bread crumbs
1 tablespoon of fennel seeds, whirred in a spice mill or crushed
1 tablespoon of cider vinegar
oil for sautéing

NOTE:
If you mix uncooked onion and garlic into sausage or meatloaf and let the mixture stand, the onion and garlic flavors become too strong. This recipe makes delicious patties, much lower in fat than traditional pork sausage. Game turkey are native to the Americas, as are all sweet and hot peppers.

HERE'S WHAT YOU DO:

Heat the oil in a skillet over medium heat. Add garlic and onion and sauté for five minutes, stirring constantly. Onions should be just translucent.
Allow to cool for five minutes.
Combine the onion mixture with the turkey, pepper flakes, cayenne, salt, sage, bread crumbs, fennel seeds, and cider vinegar. Form into six patties.
Lightly oil a skillet and brown patties over medium heat until cooked through but still moist inside (about 8 minutes). Serve immediately.

SERVES 4

BASIL (PESTO) SAUCE

🌿 THINGS YOU NEED:
2 tablespoons of walnut pieces
6 tablespoons of pignoli nuts
3 cups of tightly packed basil, leaves
3 cloves of garlic, minced
1/2 teaspoon of coarse salt
1 1/4 cups of extra virgin olive oil, divided
3/4 cup of grated Romano cheese
1/4 cup of grated Parmesan cheese
(best quality you can buy)
freshly ground black pepper

HERE'S WHAT YOU DO:

In a small skillet, lightly toast the walnuts and pignoli nuts. In a processor or blender, process the basil, nuts, garlic, salt, and 1/2 cup of olive oil for about 30 seconds. With the machine running, add the remaining oil through the feed tube and process until well blended. Add the cheeses and black pepper and process a few seconds. Serve the pesto with penne shaped pasta, or wherever pesto sauce is needed in a recipe.

NOTE: To serve 4, cook 3/4 of a pound of pasta in a generous amount of boiling salted water. While pasta is cooking, take 2 or 3 tablespoons of the boiling water and add to 3/4 cup of the sauce before tossing it with the pasta. Serve with extra Parmesan and freshly ground black pepper.

MAKES 3 CUPS

BASIC TOMATO SAUCE

❧ THINGS YOU NEED:

3 tablespoons of olive oil
1 or 2 cloves of garlic, minced or put through a garlic press
1 medium onion, chopped or grated
28 ounces of whole tomatoes in purée
6 ounces of tomato paste
1 bay leaf
2 teaspoons of chopped oregano
1 tablespoon of torn basil leaves
1 tablespoon of chopped flat leaf parsley
1/2 teaspoon of sugar
a good pinch of red pepper flakes
salt and pepper to taste
water, as needed

NOTE: The secret to tender meatballs is to use stale Italian bread that has been soaked in cold water and squeezed out, rather than bread crumbs. Sauté meatballs separately and add to the sauce to simmer.

HERE'S WHAT YOU DO:

Heat olive oil in large skillet, over medium heat. Add garlic and onion and sauté until golden. *DO NOT BROWN.* Coarsely chop the whole tomatoes just enough to break them up. Add the tomato paste to the sautéed onions. Stir to blend. Add the coarsely chopped tomatoes, bay leaf, oregano, basil, parsley, sugar, red pepper flakes, salt and pepper. Add some water if sauce seems too thick. Cover and simmer for 20 minutes, then adjust seasonings to your taste. Let simmer, covered, on lowest heat setting, for about 1 hour. You may add meatballs.

MAKES 1 TO 1 1/2 QUARTS

CRISPY POTATOES
WITH HERBS

🌿 THINGS YOU NEED:

8 large Russet or Bliss potatoes, skin on, rinsed, and cut into quarters
1/3 cup of olive oil
1 tablespoon of thyme leaves
1 tablespoon of minced oregano leaves
1 tablespoon of rosemary needles, crushed
1 large bay leaf
1 tablespoon of minced lemon sage leaves
2 cloves of garlic, peeled and sliced
freshly ground pepper
cayenne pepper
salt to taste

HERE'S WHAT YOU DO:

Preheat oven to 350° F.

Place the potatoes in a baking pan and add the olive oil to coat. Sprinkle on the thyme, oregano, rosemary, bay leaf, lemon sage, garlic, peppers, and salt to your taste. Bake for 45 minutes, shaking the pan a few times, or until the potatoes are crisp and tender. Discard the bay leaf and serve with meat, chicken, or seafood.

NOTE: *These make an excellent accompaniment to Roast Leg of Lamb (see page 14).*

THYME

SERVES 4-6

PEPPERS WITH SAGE

❧ THINGS YOU NEED:
1/3 cup of olive oil
1 clove of garlic, minced
2 tablespoons of minced sage leaves
1 tablespoon of minced oregano leaves
1 teaspoon of salt
1 1/2 teaspoons of ground pepper
2 medium red peppers, cored and sliced into thin slivers
1 medium green pepper, cored and sliced into thin slivers
1 medium yellow pepper, cored and sliced into thin slivers
1 large red onion, peeled and sliced into thin circles
sprigs of sage

HERE'S WHAT YOU DO:

Heat the olive oil in a large skillet. Add the garlic, sage, oregano, salt and pepper. Sauté 3 minutes. Add the peppers, sauté 5 minutes, stirring frequently. Add the onion, sauté 5 minutes or until limp. Peppers will remain fairly firm. Transfer to a serving dish and garnish with sprigs of sage.

NOTE: *Serve warm as a side dish with roasts or fish or serve at room temperature as a salad or appetizer.*

SERVES 4

TOMATOES, BASIL,
AND RED ONION RINGS

🌺 THINGS YOU NEED:

4 medium garden ripe tomatoes, about
5 or 6 ounces each
4 thin slices from a medium size red onion
4 large basil leaves, torn into small pieces
salt to taste
2 tablespoons of olive oil
1 tablespoon of balsamic vinegar
sprig of basil

BASIL

HERE'S WHAT YOU DO:

About 1 hour before serving, core stem ends of tomatoes; cut tomatoes into 1-inch wedges. Place in a glass bowl. Separate onion slices into rings and scatter over tomatoes, along with the basil leaves and salt. Drizzle with olive oil and balsamic vinegar. Toss lightly and leave at room temperature until serving time. Garnish with a basil sprig.

SERVES 4

CAJUN MAYONNAISE

❋ THINGS YOU NEED:

1 cup of mayonnaise
4 large cloves of garlic, minced
1/4 cup of minced cilantro leaves
1/4 cup of minced oregano leaves
1 teaspoon of ground black pepper
1 teaspoon of Chili Powder (see page 6)
1 teaspoon of dried mustard
1 teaspoon of crushed cumin seed
pinch of cayenne pepper
2 jalapeno peppers, cored, and minced
cilantro or parsley, chopped

HERE'S WHAT YOU DO:

In a small bowl, combine mayonnaise, garlic, cilantro, oregano, black pepper, chili powder, mustard, cumin seed, cayenne pepper, and jalapeno peppers. Cover and chill for at least 4 hours or overnight. Mound into a serving bowl and garnish with cilantro or parsley.

NOTE: *It is best to make this recipe 3 to 4 days before serving. The longer it sits the better it gets. Serve with crab cakes or add a dollop to a bowl of fish chowder. You can also use this as a spread on crackers or toast triangles.*

MAKES 1 CUP

HOT HERB-GARLIC BREAD

❧ THINGS YOU NEED:

14-inch loaf crusty Italian bread
1/2 cup of soft butter
2 teaspoons of minced parsley
2 teaspoons of finely snipped dillweed
2 teaspoons of chopped oregano
1 clove of garlic, finely minced or squeezed through a garlic press
Parmesan cheese, grated

HERE'S WHAT YOU DO:

Preheat oven to 400° F.

Cut bread diagonally into 1-inch slices, leaving each slice attached at the bottom of the loaf. Blend soft butter, herbs, and garlic thoroughly. Lay a piece of foil large enough to wrap completely around loaf on your cutting board or counter. Place loaf in center of foil. Using a brush or small spatula, spread butter mixture on both sides of each slice, holding the slices apart with one hand and spreading with the other.
Shape foil around loaf in a boat fashion, twisting the ends and leaving the top open. Brush any remaining butter on top and sprinkle with Parmesan cheese.
Bake for 10 minutes. Serve hot.

NOTE: This bread can be prepared ahead up to baking. It freezes exceptionally well. Wrap the foil completely around loaf. Open the top when bread is defrosted and ready to be baked. Keep one in the freezer ready to be heated when you need it in a hurry.

SERVES 4

ROSEMARY FEATHER BISCUITS

🌺 THINGS YOU NEED:

2 cups of all-purpose flour
1 teaspoon of baking soda
1/2 teaspoon of salt
1/4 cup of cold butter cut into small pieces
1/4 cup of white vinegar
1/2 cup of milk
1 tablespoon of snipped rosemary needles

NOTE: *These biscuits are feathery light and are particularly good at breakfast or tea time.*

HERE'S WHAT YOU DO:

Preheat oven to 450° F.

Sift together the flour, baking soda, and salt. Cut in butter pieces with a fork or pastry blender until the mixture resembles small peas. Combine vinegar, milk, and rosemary; add to flour mixture. Mix only until the flour is moistened. Gather dough together into a ball and knead lightly 3 or 4 times. Roll or pat out the dough until it is 1/2-inch thick. Cut the dough into mounds with a biscuit cutter dipped in flour. Bake on an ungreased baking sheet for 10-12 minutes. Serve hot!

ROSEMARY

MAKES 6-8 2 1/2-INCH BISCUITS

BAY LEAF FLAVORED
CUSTARD SAUCE

❋ THINGS YOU NEED:

1 1/3 cups of low-fat milk
3 fresh bay leaves, torn in half
2 whole eggs
1 tablespoon of sugar
pinch of salt
scented geranium leaf
or strip of orange rind, knotted

NOTE: Try this sauce over fresh blueberries or peeled sliced ripe peaches!
NOTE: 1/2 cup of egg substitute can replace 2 whole eggs. The custard will take longer to thicken.

HERE'S WHAT YOU DO:

Bring water to boil in the bottom of a double boiler. In a small pan, add bay leaves to the milk and heat until milk is scalded. In a small bowl, combine the eggs, sugar, and salt. Whisk scalded milk mixture gradually into the egg mixture. Pour into top of the double boiler set over the boiling water. Cook, whisking, until the mixture thickens and coats a metal spoon. Remove from heat and pour custard into a glass bowl to cool. Remove bay leaves before serving over fresh fruit. Garnish, if desired, with a scented geranium leaf or a strip of orange rind, knotted.

SERVES 4

ORANGE GERANIUM PECAN COOKIES

NOTE: This recipe makes a not-too-sweet cookie that uses whole wheat flour and scented geranium leaves. They're a pleasing addition to fresh fruit or sherbet as a dessert.

❋ THINGS YOU NEED:

1/2 cup of butter
1/2 cup of sugar
1 egg
2 tablespoons of chopped orange geranium leaves
1/2 teaspoon of grated orange rind
1/2 teaspoon of orange extract
1 cup of unbleached all-purpose flour
1/2 cup of whole wheat flour
1 1/4 teaspoons of baking powder
1 cup of (approximately) very finely chopped pecans or pecan meal

HERE'S WHAT YOU DO:

In a medium size mixing bowl, cream together the butter and sugar. Beat in the egg, then the orange geranium leaves, orange rind, and orange extract. Sift together the flours and baking powder and stir into the creamed mixture. Cover dough and chill in refrigerator for two hours or more. *Preheat oven to 375° F.* (You can make the dough in the morning and bake it late in the day.) Scoop up about 1/2 tablespoon of the chilled dough and form it into a 2-inch long log. Roll in the pecans and arrange on an ungreased, 17x14-inch cookie sheet. You should get 7 rows of 6 cookies each. Bake for 10-12 minutes or until the bottoms of cookies are light brown. Remove immediately to a cooling rack.

MAKES 40-42 COOKIES

SHERRY PEPPER

🌶 THINGS YOU NEED:

1 fifth of inexpensive dry sherry
10 dried hot peppers

HERE'S WHAT YOU DO:

Add the peppers to the sherry. Recap the bottle and store in a cool, dark place for a couple of weeks or longer.

NOTE: *Be sure to make this recipe ahead of time. Use the sherry pepper to perk up soups, sauces, and Bloody Marys. It keeps indefinitely. Pour some into recycled soy sauce bottles with shaker tops for easy dispensing. If you don't have the sherry pepper, add a tablespoon of dry sherry and 1/4 teaspoon of hot pepper flakes to the drink.*

MAKES 1 FIFTH GALLON

HOT MINTED CHOCOLATE

❦ THINGS YOU NEED:

1/4 cup of cocoa
4 tablespoons of sugar
3 sprigs of fresh mint
pinch of salt
1/4 cup of water
2 1/4 cups of milk
sprigs of mint

HERE'S WHAT YOU DO:

In a medium saucepan, whisk together the cocoa, sugar, 3 mint sprigs, salt, and water. Allow to steep for 30 minutes. Place over medium heat, and gradually add the milk, stirring constantly. Simmer over low heat for about 10 minutes, stirring frequently. Discard the mint leaves and pour into cups. Garnish with fresh sprigs of mint and serve.

NOTE: *Pour this over a few ice cubes in a tall glass. It leaves you feeling wonderfully refreshed and energized.*

SERVES 4

INDEX

African Slave Trade	1	Lamb	
Apples		Roast Leg of	14, 19
Granny Smith	13	Mediterranean cooking	1
Balsamic vinegar	21	Nutrition	1
Barbecue Blend	6	Oswego Indians	5
Biscuits		Peaches	25
Feather	24	Peppers with Sage	20
Bloody Mary	27	Pesto Sauce	17
Blueberries	25	Pork Chops	13
Bouquet Garni	6	Potatoes	
Breads		Russet	19
Garlic	23	Bliss	19
Italian	18	Salads	
Toast Crisps	8	Tomato	21
Chicken		Sauces	
Roasted with Pesto	15	Basil	17
Chiffonade	4	Custard	25
Chocolate, Hot Minted	28	Pesto	17
Cottage Cheese	7	Tomato	18
Cookies		Scallops, Curried	11
Orange Geranium Pecan	26	Sherry, Dry	27
Crab Cakes	22	Simmons, Amelia	1
Dressing		Soups	
Cajun Mayonnaise	22	Carrot Orange	9
Fines Herbes	6	Chowder	22
Fish		Lentil	10
Shark	12	Turkey Sausage	16
French Provincial	1	World War II	1
Garden	2	Yogurt	9
Herbs			
bergamot	5		
drying	5		
hints	4		
Mexican	6		
of Provence	1		
tea time	24		
vinegars	5		

Neat Pocket Cookbooks from
BRICK TOWER PRESS

Forthcoming Titles
Pumpkin

MAIL ORDER AND GENERAL INFORMATION

Many of our titles are carried by your local book store or gift and museum shop. If they do not already carry our line please ask them to write us for information.

If you are unable to purchase our pocket cookbook titles from your local shop, call or write to us. They are available through mail order. Just send us a check or money order for $4.00 per title, shipping and handling included, to the address below or call us Monday through Friday, 9 AM to 5 PM, EST. We accept Visa and Mastercard.

Send all mail order, book club, and special sales requests to the address below or call us for a free catalog. We can mail our catalog to you or e-mail a paper-free copy. In any case we would like to hear from you.

Brick Tower Press
1230 Park Avenue, 10th Floor
New York, NY 10128

Telephone & Facsimile
1-212-427-7139
1-800-68-BRICK

E-mail
bricktower@aol.com

CPSIA information can be obtained
at www.ICGtesting.com
Printed in the USA
LVHW091029140419
614124LV00002B/579/P